## WEEKLY WR READER®
### EARLY LEARNING LIBRARY

# STORMS
# HAILSTORMS

**by Jim Mezzanotte**
**Reading consultant:** Susan Nations, M.Ed.,
author/literacy coach/consultant in literacy development

**Science and curriculum consultant:** Debra Voege, M.A.,
science and math curriculum resource teacher

**Please visit our web site at: www.garethstevens.com**
**For a free color catalog describing Weekly Reader® Early Learning Library's**
**list of high-quality books, call 1-877-445-5824 (USA) or 1-800-387-3178 (Canada).**
**Weekly Reader® Early Learning Library's fax: (414) 336-0164.**

**Library of Congress Cataloging-in-Publication Data**

Mezzanotte, Jim.
    Hailstorms / by Jim Mezzanotte.
       p. cm. — (Storms)
    Includes bibliographical references and index.
    ISBN-13: 978-0-8368-7912-4 (lib. bdg.)
    ISBN-13: 978-0-8368-7919-3 (softcover)
    1. Hailstorms—Juvenile literature. 2. Hail—Juvenile literature. I. Title.
  QC929.H15M49 2007
  551.55'4—dc22
                                  2006033920

This edition first published in 2007 by
**Weekly Reader® Early Learning Library**
A Member of the WRC Media Family of Companies
330 West Olive Street, Suite 100
Milwaukee, WI 53212 USA

Copyright © 2007 by Weekly Reader® Early Learning Library

Editorial direction: Mark Sachner
Editor: Barbara Kiely Miller
Art direction, cover and layout design: Tammy West
Photo research: Diane Laska-Swanke

Photo credits: Cover, title, pp. 5, 7, 18 © AP Images; pp. 6, 11, 13, 19, 21 © Weatherpix Stock Images; p. 8 © Jim Reed/CORBIS; p. 10 © Adam Jones/Visuals Unlimited; pp. 12, 14 Scott M. Krall/© Weekly Reader Early Learning Library; p. 15 © Jeff J. Daly/Visuals Unlimited; p. 17 © Jim Reed/Photo Researchers, Inc.

Printed in the United States of America

1 2 3 4 5 6 7 8 9 10 10 09 08 07 06

# Table of Contents

**Cover and title page:** A truck slows down as hail falls on a Missouri road. The hailstorm brought cars and trucks to a stop and caused many accidents.

# CHAPTER 1

## Here Comes Hail!

Have you ever seen hail? On a warm day, dark storm clouds appear. You wait for raindrops, but something else falls from the sky. They look like small, white stones. They make a clicking sound on the street. Hail is falling!

Hailstones are not rocks. They are pieces of ice. Many hailstones can fall in a short time. They make it hard to see anything.

When they stop falling, you look around. It is a spring day, but ice covers the ground! The hailstones melt quickly. In a short time, they are gone.

In Colorado, hailstones the size of golf balls cover the grass at a golf course.

Thunderstorms bring rain that farmers need and the chance of lightning and hail. Lightning strikes the ground near this farm.

Hail falls during **thunderstorms**. Most parts of the world have these storms. They form in warm, **humid** weather. In the United States, they mostly form in spring and summer.

Rain usually falls during thunderstorms, but hail can fall, too. The storms also produce **thunder** and **lightning**. In some places, a **tornado** may form.

Hail mostly falls in places that do not become very cold or very hot.

In the United States, hail mostly falls in the middle of the country. Hail often falls in high places. Colorado has many high mountains and gets a lot of hail.

Other parts of the world get hail, too. Both China and India get hail.

In Colorado, people at a golf match take shelter during a hailstorm.

Hailstones can be many different sizes. They can be as tiny as a pea. They can be larger, like a golf ball. Some hailstones are as large as a melon!

Hail can cause a lot of damage. It can break windows. It can flatten **crops**. Large hailstones can hurt or kill animals. Sometimes, they can hurt people, too.

This hailstone is almost twice as big as a baseball.

# CHAPTER 2

## Hailstorms in Action

Hail forms inside a thundercloud. But how does a thundercloud form? First, the Sun warms air near the ground.

White, puffy clouds continue to grow larger in the sky. Soon they will turn into storm clouds.

This air is full of water. The water is not a liquid. It is a colorless **gas** called water vapor.

The warm air rises from the ground. Higher in the sky, the air cools. The water vapor cools, too. It turns into water drops. The drops join together. They begin forming a cloud.

As the warm air rises, it pulls up more warm air. More water drops join together, making bigger drops. The cloud keeps growing.

The cloud reaches up into the sky. It is thousands of feet tall. It is dark, because it is full of water drops. When the drops become big and heavy, they begin to fall.

Rising air stretches this storm cloud as it turns darker. This storm dropped hailstones the size of baseballs.

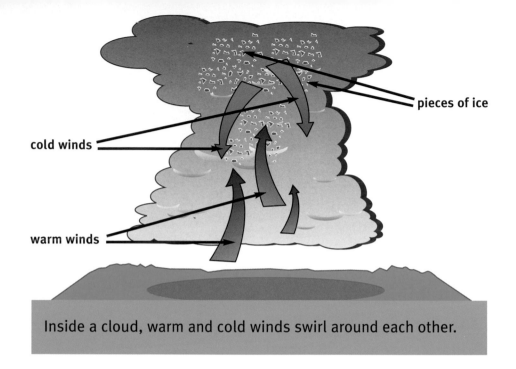

cold winds

warm winds

pieces of ice

Inside a cloud, warm and cold winds swirl around each other.

The top of the cloud is colder than the bottom. At the top, water freezes into tiny pieces of ice. These pieces begin falling, too.

Inside the cloud, strong winds blow. Cold winds blow down from the top. At the same time, warm air keeps rising. So warm winds blow up from the bottom of the cloud.

In the bottom of the cloud, raindrops hit the pieces of ice. The drops freeze around the ice, forming hailstones.

The hailstones move up and down inside the cloud, blown by the warm and cold winds.

Inside this storm cloud, rain freezes around small pieces of ice. The cloud drops rain and large hail on Texas crops.

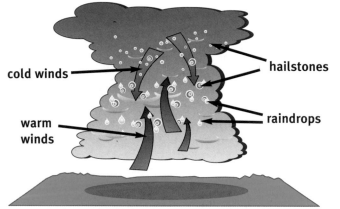

cold winds

hailstones

warm winds

raindrops

The hailstones may stay in the cloud for ten minutes. Sometimes, they move up and down more than twenty times.

As hailstones move inside the cloud, more raindrops freeze around them. They are covered with more layers of ice. With each layer, they grow bigger.

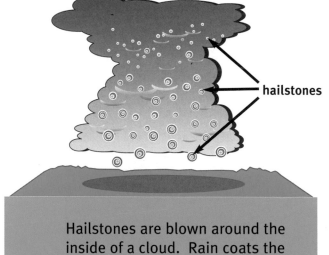

hailstones

Hailstones are blown around the inside of a cloud. Rain coats the hailstones, making them bigger.

Finally, the hailstones become too heavy. The winds cannot hold them up. They begin to fall.

Some hailstones are very tiny. They melt before reaching the ground. Other hailstones are larger. They cover the ground.

If you cut a hailstone in half, you will see many rings. Each ring is a layer of ice.

Inside each hailstone are rings of ice. The rings surround a tiny piece of ice in the center of the hailstone.

# CHAPTER 3

## Huge Hailstorms

Hailstones are hard balls of ice. They fall to the ground very fast. They can travel faster than a car. When they hit, watch out!

Every year, hail damages thousands of homes and cars.
Hail smashed the window of this car.

Sometimes, hail falls on farm fields. It smashes into plants, breaking them apart. Farmers lose their crops.

Hail also falls on cars. It dents the metal and breaks windshields. Hail falls on buildings, too. It breaks windows and smashes roofs.

These people run for cover when a hailstorm delays a race.

Bigger hailstones may do the most harm.
They are like cannonballs from the sky! Small
animals get hurt or killed by them. Big animals
get hurt, too.

Hail does not often hurt people. When it
does, the hailstones are very large. These large
hailstones do not fall very often.

When a thunderstorm forms, a lot can happen. Besides hail, heavy rain may fall. The rain can cause floods. Hail can make flooding worse. It clogs up places where the water would drain.

Strong winds may blow. They can blow hail in different directions. Thunderstorms produce tornadoes, too. Sometimes, hail falls just before a tornado hits!

A giant thunderstorm hangs over western Oklahoma. It might spin tornadoes or throw down huge hailstones.

# CHAPTER 4

## Hail Safety

During a hailstorm, scientists use a **rain gauge** to measure the rain.  The rain falls into this tube. Marks on it show how many inches of rain fell. Scientists use a ruler to measure hailstones.

What should you do when hail starts falling? The best place to stay safe is in your home. Outside, you could get hit by hailstones.  Hail also makes the ground very slippery.

Some people cover up their cars and boats. If they can, they bring bikes and other things inside. They try not to drive on the slippery roads. Hail could also break windshields.

From safe inside your home, you can watch the hailstones fall. It is an amazing sight!

Hail covers a highway in New Mexico. Drivers try to stay off the road when hail falls.

# Glossary

**crops** — plants that people grow for food

**gas** — a form that something can take, such as water. Unlike a solid, a gas cannot hold its own shape. It keeps spreading out. Usually, a gas cannot be seen.

**humid** — having a lot of water vapor in the air

**lightning** — a huge amount of electricity that flashes through the air

**rain gauge** — a container for collecting and measuring rainfall

**thunder** — the sound of exploding air near a lightning bolt

**thunderstorms** — storms that bring thunder and lightning, heavy rain, and hail. They can also bring strong winds, including tornadoes.

**tornado** — a spinning tube of wind that reaches down to the ground from clouds. It sucks things up and spits them out.

# For More Information

## Books

*Forecasting the Weather.* Watching the Weather (series). Elizabeth Miles (Heinemann)

*Hail.* Extreme Weather (series). Liza N. Burby (Rosen)

*Ice Storms and Hailstorms.* Nature on the Rampage (series). Duncan Scheff (Raintree)

*W is for Wind: A Weather Alphabet.* Pat Michaels (Sleeping Bear Press)

## Web Site

**Weather Wiz Kids: Weather Instruments**
*www.weatherwizkids.com/wxinstruments.htm*
Learn about the different instruments used to measure the weather. Read about different kinds of storms.

**Publisher's note to educators and parents:** Our editors have carefully reviewed this Web site to ensure that it is suitable for children. Many Web sites change frequently, however, and we cannot guarantee that a site's future contents will continue to meet our high standards of quality and educational value. Be advised that children should be closely supervised whenever they access the Internet.

# Index

# About the Author

**Jim Mezzanotte** has written many books for children. He lives in Milwaukee, Wisconsin, with his wife and two sons. He has always been interested in the weather, especially big storms.